28 DAYS

MOMENTS IN BLACK HISTORY THAT CHANGED THE WORLD

CHARLES R. SMITH JR.

ILLUSTRATED BY

SHANE W. EVANS

A NEAL PORTER BOOK
ROARING BROOK PRESS
NEW YORK

For Sabine, Adrian, and Sebastian. Know your history.
—C.S.

Thank you God for this gift.
Thank you to the "Chocolate Team" for another step in the direction of positive.
Thanks to my family for supporting me in this work. Love y'all.
—S.W.E.

Text copyright © 2015 by Charles R. Smith
Illustrations copyright © 2015 by Shane Evans
A Neal Porter Book
Published by Roaring Brook Press
Roaring Brook Press is a division of Holtzbrinck Publishing Holdings Limited Partnership
175 Fifth Avenue, New York, New York 10010
The artwork for this book was created using mixed medium collage, oil, and digital techniques.
mackids.com

Library of Congress Cataloging-in-Publication Data

Smith, Charles R., Jr., 1969–
    28 days : moments in Black history that changed the world / Charles
Smith, Shane Evans. — First edition.
        pages cm
    "A Neal Porter book."
Summary: "A picture book look at many of the men and women who
revolutionized life for African Americans throughout history"— Provided
by publisher.
Audience: Ages 4 to 10.
    ISBN 978-1-59643-820-0 (hardcover)
1. African Americans—History—Juvenile literature. 2. African
Americans—Biography—Juvenile literature. 3. Heroes—United
States—Biography—Juvenile literature. 4. Successful people—United
States—Biography—Juvenile literature. I. Evans, Shane, illustrator.
II. Title. III. Title: Twenty-eight days.
E185.S5812 2015
    973'.0496073—dc23

                                                                    2014009898

Roaring Brook Press books may be purchased for business or promotional use. For information on bulk purchases
please contact Macmillan Corporate and Premium Sales Department at (800) 221-7945 x5442
or by email at specialmarkets@macmillan.com.

First edition 2015
Book design by Jennifer Browne
Printed in China by Toppan Leefung Printing Ltd., Dongguan City, Guangdong Province

3   5   7   9   10   8   6   4

A Note from the Author

I've always had a love-hate relationship with Black History Month.

I love that black culture is shared and studied for a whole month, but as a student of color, I hated the idea of ignoring it the other eleven months. On top of that, I kept learning the same things about the same people and after a while, no matter how proud I was of my culture, I got bored and just stopped listening.

As an author, I wanted to change that.

I wanted to bring Black History Month alive. I wanted to go beyond the familiar names and faces I saw every year without new additions. I wanted to show the variety of accomplishments black people have achieved, not just in the long ago past, but in recent times and present day, as well. Ultimately, I wanted to provide a wealth of information for teachers and students alike all in one book.

So I created this book, *28 Days*. But the idea was not my own. My insightful editor, Neal Porter, reached out to me with the idea of doing a book on Black History Month centered around the number twenty-eight. It was my job to flesh out the concept with twenty-eight subjects tied together into one cohesive unit. And considering the number of achievements in Black History, this would not be easy.

So I started from the beginning, when our country was "born", in 1776. A name I was introduced to as a child, Crispus Attucks, would be the first. I decided to end in the present, with our first black president, Barack Obama. In between I hunted for unfamiliar names with great stories and accomplishments. This included, but wasn't limited to, Robert Smalls, who stole a boat from Confederate sailors and delivered it to the Union. This included the first black astronauts, Guy Bluford and Mae Jemison, who I came across in school as a young aspiring astronaut myself, looking for "new names in Black History" on my own.

I also made a point of including laws that directly affected black people. From the dreadful, such as the Dred Scott decision, to the hopeful, such as Brown vs. Board of Education. But you'll also notice there are twenty-nine days, not just twenty-eight. This is because Black History Month happens in February and there are sometimes twenty-nine days due to leap year. The final "day" serves as a reminder to readers that great things can happen on any day to anyone, including them, if they are determined enough and work hard.

The book is rounded out with familiar names and faces in Black History to create what I hope becomes an indispensable tool to teachers and provides endless inspiration, not just for people of color, but anyone with a thirst for knowledge.

. . . and the Artist

The process of creating this book was like "stealing away" into time. I am now able to better see these events that I have heard stories about for so long. As an artist I am often looking through a lens of love that shows me so much good in the world in both good and bad times. This book means "Love Almighty!" to me as a person. It is like a rock, and I am comforted knowing that this is where we stand in this journey. I am honored to have been a part of it.

Day 1

MARCH 5, 1770

Crispus Attucks
is shot by a British
soldier, beginning the Boston Massacre
and, ultimately, the Revolutionary War.

Crispus Attucks
was a man, self-made,
Crispus Attucks
was a man, unafraid.

When the redcoats turned
on the colonists with guns,
Crispus Attucks stood tall
and challenged each one.

One shot,
two shots
straight to the chest,
Crispus Attucks went down,
his heart put to rest.

A slave,
a sailor,
a patriot was he,
Crispus Attucks struck
the first blow for liberty.

First to defy,
first to die,
Crispus Attucks sacrificed
for the flag we hold high.

*Crispus Attucks was born a slave in 1723
in Framingham, Massachusetts. He was the
property of William Brown but the son of an
African father and a Native American mother.
In 1750, he ran away to work on whaling ships,
but also worked on the docks and as a rope
maker. The British troops ("redcoats") competed
with the colonists for jobs, usually offering to
work for less money. This led to friction and
arguments between the troops and colonists.
Crispus and four other men were shot that
day and their deaths became a spark for the
Revolutionary War.*

MARCH 6, 1857 Dred Scott decision,

denying the right of citizenship to black people after slavery ended.

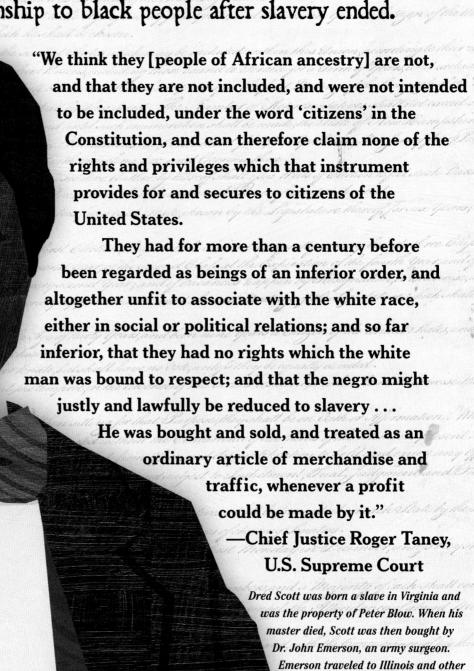

"We think they [people of African ancestry] are not, and that they are not included, and were not intended to be included, under the word 'citizens' in the Constitution, and can therefore claim none of the rights and privileges which that instrument provides for and secures to citizens of the United States.

They had for more than a century before been regarded as beings of an inferior order, and altogether unfit to associate with the white race, either in social or political relations; and so far inferior, that they had no rights which the white man was bound to respect; and that the negro might justly and lawfully be reduced to slavery . . . He was bought and sold, and treated as an ordinary article of merchandise and traffic, whenever a profit could be made by it."

—Chief Justice Roger Taney, U.S. Supreme Court

Dred Scott was born a slave in Virginia and was the property of Peter Blow. When his master died, Scott was then bought by Dr. John Emerson, an army surgeon. Emerson traveled to Illinois and other parts of the modern-day Midwest, taking Scott with him. Emerson also died, so Scott went back to Mrs. Emerson to purchase his freedom for $300 because he lived for a time in Illinois, a free state. She refused. Scott then took his case to court to purchase his freedom under the premise that he was a citizen of the United States.

Day 3

May 13, 1862 **Robert Smalls**, a slave in the Confederate crew on a ship, commandeers it, sails it north and delivers it to the Union.

Under cloak of night, *Planter* disappears; stolen to freedom.

Robert Smalls became a wheelman (ship's pilot) and eventually a captain for the Union during the Civil War. He was the first black captain of an American ship and ultimately achieved the rank of major general. Robert was unable to read or write but that did not stop him from speaking with President Abraham Lincoln about the Union using slaves in the military. He became a popular speaker and took that skill into politics where he served five terms in the U.S. Congress working for the rights of blacks.

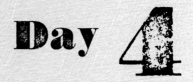

Day 4

July 9, 1868 14th Amendment
to the Constitution overturns the
Dred Scott decision.

14th Amendment
Section 1.

"All persons born or naturalized in the United States,
and subject to the jurisdiction thereof,
are citizens of the United States
and of the State wherein they reside."

July 9, 1893 Daniel Hale Williams successfully performs first heart operation, before the inventions of penicillin, antibiotics, or X-rays.

Stab-wounded heart fills
chest with blood. No medicine;
doctor is tested.
Chest incision reveals heart;
with calm, doctor reveals skill.

Daniel Hale Williams received his medical degree from Chicago Medical College in 1883. Upset that black people were not allowed treatment in most hospitals, he opened Provident Hospital in Chicago, Illinois. Provident accepted doctors and patients of all colors. When James Cornish, a black man, came into the hospital with a stab wound to the chest, Dr. Williams concluded after observation that Mr. Cornish had internal chest bleeding. Using new sterile techniques, Dr. Williams was able to avoid internal infection and James Cornish would live another twenty years.

Day 6

May 18, 1896 *Plessy v. Ferguson* decision, stating that separate but equal facilities were fair.

"That [the Separate Car Act] does not conflict with the Thirteenth Amendment, which abolished slavery . . . is too clear for argument . . . A statute which implies merely a legal distinction between the white and colored races—a distinction which is founded in the color of the two races, and which must always exist so long as white men are distinguished from the other race by color—has no tendency to destroy the legal equality of the two races . . .

The object of the [Fourteenth] Amendment was undoubtedly to enforce the absolute equality of the two races before the law, but, in the nature of things, it could not have been intended to abolish distinctions based upon color, or to enforce social, as distinguished from political, equality, or a commingling of the two races upon terms unsatisfactory to either."

When Homer Plessy, a black shoemaker, tried to sit in the white portion of a railroad car, he was asked to leave because of his skin color. He refused and was arrested. Plessy decided to sue, arguing he was protected under the 13th and 14th Amendments. His case started in New Orleans and progressed all the way to the U.S. Supreme Court.

Day 7

APRIL 6, 1909 **Matthew Henson**

and Robert Peary reach

the North Pole, the first men

to ever do so.

Maripahluk, "the kind one"
Adventurous
Tenacious
Teacher
Historic
Educated
World Traveler

Matthew Henson was orphaned at age thirteen. From then on he traveled the world, starting on a steamship from Baltimore. At age twenty-one, Matthew met Naval Lieutenant Robert Peary at a hat store when his boss recommended him for a job on an expedition to Central America. Many expeditions later, Henson and Peary attempted to reach the North Pole. It took several attempts before they were successful. Upon their return home, they were treated as frauds when another explorer claimed he had reached the North Pole first. More than a year later, their claim was proved true and Peary was given many honors and medals. Henson received nothing and was not recognized until 1944. Maripahluk was the name given to him by the Inuit Eskimos.

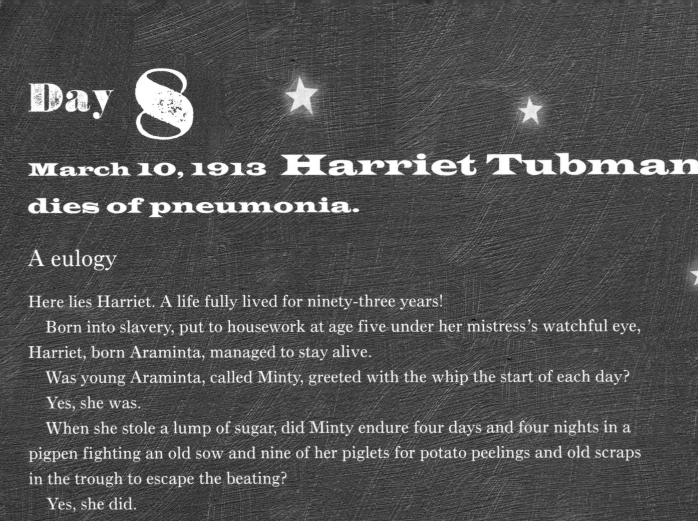

Day 8

March 10, 1913 Harriet Tubman dies of pneumonia.

A eulogy

Here lies Harriet. A life fully lived for ninety-three years!

Born into slavery, put to housework at age five under her mistress's watchful eye, Harriet, born Araminta, managed to stay alive.

Was young Araminta, called Minty, greeted with the whip the start of each day?

Yes, she was.

When she stole a lump of sugar, did Minty endure four days and four nights in a pigpen fighting an old sow and nine of her piglets for potato peelings and old scraps in the trough to escape the beating?

Yes, she did.

Did Minty endure a blow to the head that cracked her skull, giving her a lifetime of headaches, blackouts, and visions? Visions she felt were messages from God.

Stunning visions of flying and freedom. Terrifying visions of hoofbeats and mothers screaming as their babies are stolen away.

Minty endured. Oh yes, sister Harriet endured.

And that endurance was tested as she dreamed of freedom, the dream growing stronger each day after her sisters were sold away.

Araminta Ross soon became Harriet Tubman when she took her mother's first name and her husband's last name, and Harriet was no longer a child but a young woman. Oh, how sister Harriet yearned for freedom!

And if you knew Harriet like I knew her, you would know that she believed there was one of two things she had a right to, liberty or death; if she couldn't have one, she would have the other.

Through the guidance and kindness of others, she escaped Maryland a slave and entered Pennsylvania a free woman. The joy that glorious golden day was a nectar Harriet knew others had to taste. So rather than enjoy all that sweet freedom alone, sister Harriet soon found herself running back home to deliver her family from slavery. A task she accomplished, which was no small feat, a task she would then continue to repeat. From south to north, she delivered slaves, guiding them at night under the stars gaze. Any slaves on the journey who wanted to retreat had a pistol pointed at them as Harriet silenced them.

Celebrated in the North, a wanted criminal in the South, Harriet continued. But as the years passed she took care of others, especially the elderly, including her father and mother.

Harriet we salute you, courageous and brave. Harriet we find strength in you, always unafraid.

Harriet Tubman was known for her work as a "conductor" with the Underground Railroad, which was not an actual railroad but a network of people and trails used to help slaves escape to the North where slavery was illegal. Through the use of song, slaves were able to communicate with each other. Through the use of quilts, slaves were able to know which houses were "safe" for them to approach for help. Harriet became very skilled at leading slaves north and took pride in "never losing a passenger." Harriet's skill was put to use in the Civil War where she worked as a nurse, a cook, and a spy. Working with slaves, Harriet got information about the Confederate army that led to many Union victories. For all her help during the Civil War, Harriet Tubman was buried with full military honors in Auburn, New York.

May 15, 1918 Henry Johnson single-handedly fights off a platoon of Germans in the Argonne Forest during World War I to keep his friend Needham Roberts from being captured.

To Europe, Private Henry Lincoln Johnson was sent
to join "The Harlem Hellfighters," an all-black regiment.

Kept on the sidelines by the U.S. Army,
the Hellfighters saw action with the French military.

Private Henry Johnson saw action one night,
standing watch, when ambushed by Germans in a fight.

Bullets from the east, bullets from the west,
two bullets caught Private Johnson in the chest.

By Henry's side, Private Needham Roberts fought,
the two hit with grenades, stabbed, and shot.

Bloodied but not dead, Private Roberts didn't drop.
Wounded twenty-one times, Private Johnson didn't stop.

Grenades exploded, his bolo knife sliced
as Private Johnson fought for his and his friend's life.

Eight critically wounded and four dead Germans lay,
the commander included, so the enemy ran away.

The Harlem Hellfighter lived up to his name
and returned home to a hero's acclaim.

For his heroic act, Henry Johnson was the first American to receive the Croix de Guerre, the highest French military honor. Instead of going home to rest, Henry elected to stay with his squad. The United States awarded him the Distinguished Cross more than seventy-four years after his death. Upon his discharge, he was not given his disability allowance and eventually died penniless. Despite rumors that he was buried in an unmarked grave, Henry Lincoln Johnson was buried in Arlington National Cemetery with other American war heroes.

Day 10

May 25, 1919 Madam C. J. Walker dies as the richest black woman in America.

A eulogy

Friends, we are gathered here today to pay our respects and put to rest sister C. J. Walker, known to the world as Madam C. J., born to her parents as Sarah Breedlove.

Sarah was the fifth child in her family. Her brothers and sisters were born into slavery while Sarah was the first child born free. But even though she was free, little Sarah worked like a slave.

Like so many before her, Sarah worked the cotton fields in Louisiana from sunup to sundown. When she was just five, Sarah pressed on after the loss of her mother and continued to press on when her father died just two years later.

Sarah would leave Louisiana and move to Mississippi with her sister seeking greener pastures, but what she found in Mississippi was no better than what she left. At ten years old, Sarah took in laundry to earn money. Load after load, day after day, Sarah pressed on.

By fourteen Sarah had a husband and just three years later they had a baby girl they named Lelia. Now, Sarah's husband was a good man, but he passed away early, leaving Sarah and Lelia behind. But Sarah pressed on and soon was on the move again, this time heading up the Mississippi River to St. Louis to see her three brothers who owned a barbershop.

Sarah found comfort in the local church where she met well-off, educated black women who preached self-help, charity, and education. The members welcomed her and little Lelia with open arms and inspired Sarah to work even harder.

A marriage at age twenty-six that ended before it even started only strengthened Sarah's resolve, but the stresses of life were catching up to her as her hair began to thin and disappear.

Now, Sarah was a proud woman. She wanted a better life for herself and her daughter, but she didn't like what she saw in the mirror so she looked to do something about it. And she started with her hair.

Sarah came across some hair care products that grew her hair out nice and thick, and like Samson long before her, Sarah found strength in her hair. She began selling those hair care products for the company and earned more money that first week than she ever did in one week doing laundry.

With a confident head on her shoulders, Sarah took matters into her own hands by creating her own hair care products inspired by mother Africa.

Sarah perfected her formula using vegetables, natural oils, and perfumes gotten from the pharmacy and then set out selling confidence, door to door, day after day, mile after mile.

It was about this time Sarah would marry Charles J. Walker. Now, Sarah may not have gone to business school but she was smart enough to know that if you treated yourself as a high-class professional, then others would do the same. Born Sarah Breedlove but known to the world as Madam C. J. Walker.

Did Sarah tell black women they had "bad hair"? No, she did not.

Did Sarah use some high-fashion models to promote her products? No, she did not.

No friends, Sarah put her own face on her products, showing a proud black face with a confident smile to the world. Her confidence inspired others and just as she had sold products for the company that gave her better hair, Sarah offered her customers the same thing and her business took off, providing her with immense wealth. Enough to build her own factory on her own land in Pittsburgh. Enough to build another factory in Indianapolis with a beautiful movie theater because the local segregated theater charged blacks more than whites. Enough to give to charities as she pleased. Enough to build her own home in New York.

Even though she tooled around town in her fancy cars, wearing her expensive clothes and hats and furs, Madam C. J. Walker, born Sarah Breedlove, in Delta, Louisiana, never forgot where she came from. And as she traveled this great country telling her story, Sarah would remind everyone, including the great Booker T. Washington: "I came from the cotton fields in the South. I was promoted from there to the washtub . . . from there I promoted myself

into the business of making hair goods . . . I know how to grow hair as well as I know how to grow cotton."

Yes, she did. Sarah surely did.

And as I stand here before all of your tear-stained faces, I say let us remember Sarah for her generosity of spirit. Let us remember Sarah for her compassion. Let us remember Madam C. J. Walker as that little girl in the cotton fields, head covered by a handkerchief, pressing on as so many did before her.

Sarah, you may be gone, but we, too, will press on.

When Madam C. J. Walker died, her wealth was estimated at over a million dollars. She was the wealthiest black woman in the country at the time and one of the wealthiest black Americans. She took great pride in building her company and spent as much time donating money to various organizations like the NAACP to support causes concerning the black community.

June 15, 1921 Bessie Coleman

receives her pilot's license in France

since no American flight schools accepted women or blacks.

Bessie Coleman was a dreamer
from Waxahachie,
she dreamed one day
she would be somebody.
Bessie was smart,
she had education,
she loved to read books
and solve number equations.

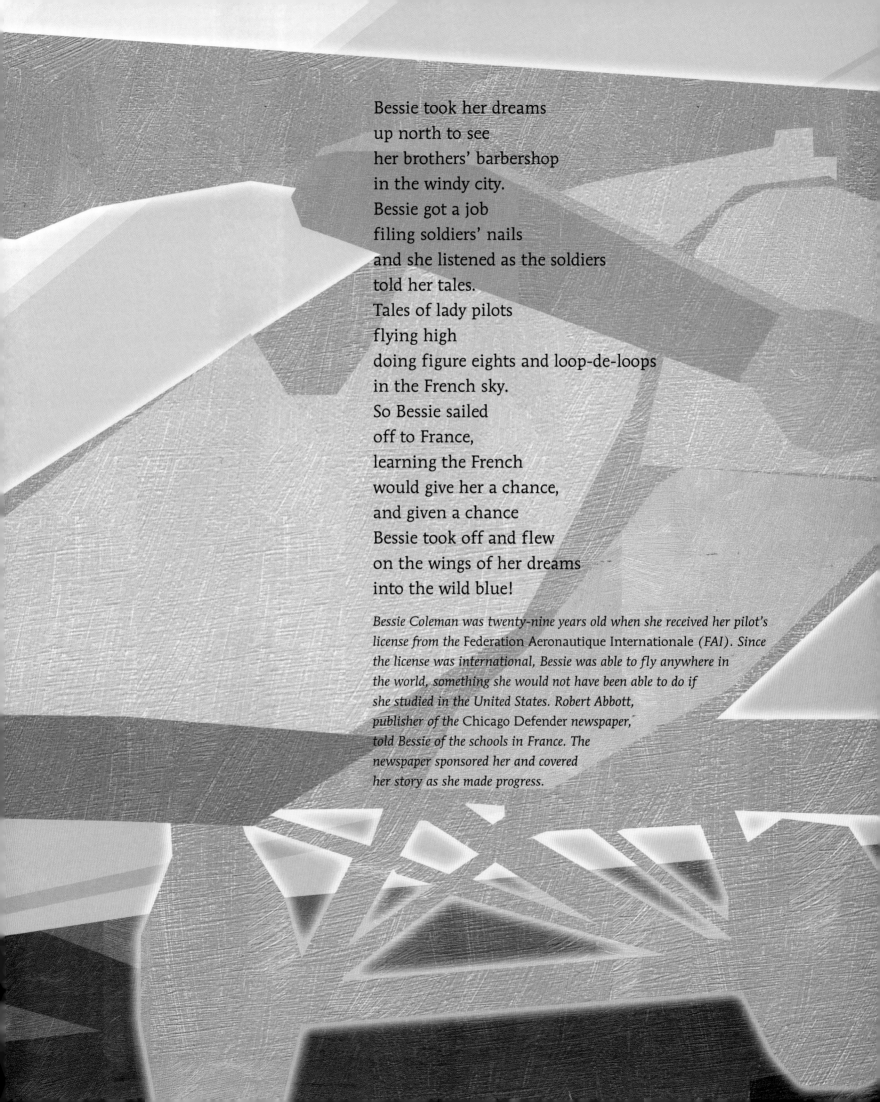

Bessie took her dreams
up north to see
her brothers' barbershop
in the windy city.
Bessie got a job
filing soldiers' nails
and she listened as the soldiers
told her tales.
Tales of lady pilots
flying high
doing figure eights and loop-de-loops
in the French sky.
So Bessie sailed
off to France,
learning the French
would give her a chance,
and given a chance
Bessie took off and flew
on the wings of her dreams
into the wild blue!

*Bessie Coleman was twenty-nine years old when she received her pilot's
license from the Federation Aeronautique Internationale (FAI). Since
the license was international, Bessie was able to fly anywhere in
the world, something she would not have been able to do if
she studied in the United States. Robert Abbott,
publisher of the Chicago Defender newspaper,
told Bessie of the schools in France. The
newspaper sponsored her and covered
her story as she made progress.*

Day 12

August 9, 1936 Jesse Owens
wins his fourth Olympic gold medal.

The eyes of Hitler
focus in on the track
on Olympian Jesse Owens,
American and black.

The son of a sharecropper
and grandson of a slave
lines up in the starting block
as the Nazi flag waves.

Eyes focus forward,
feet ready to run,
then the Buckeye Bullet
explodes at the gun.

Three winning races
and one long jump victory
earn four gold medals
and a place in history.

*Jesse Owens was the first American track-and-field athlete to win four gold medals
in a single Olympics. He tied the world record in the 100-meter dash, set an Olympic
record in the 200, set Olympic and world records in the first leg of the 4 x 100
relay, and set an Olympic record in the long jump. His record-breaking feat proved
that black athletes could compete at the highest level of the sport. He was born in
Alabama, but raised in Ohio, which is where his nickname, the Buckeye Bullet,
came from.*

Day 13

April 9, 1939, Easter Sunday *Marian Anderson* performs at Lincoln Memorial.

Lincoln looms large over a sepia songbird chirping a
                                                 sweet
sound over a sea of 75,000 inspired faces,
made up of various races.

Wide eyes witness a historic first,
while millions of ears become immersed
when the songbird's voice spreads across the
                                                 land
through the power of radio.

Souls stir as the songbird floats
on heavenly high notes
filled with the promise
                                                 of
freedom, justice, equality, and
                                                 liberty.

The pride of Philadelphia,
born of humble beginnings,
Marian Anderson stands majestic, the eldest
                                                 of
three female siblings.

The self-taught songbird sang for kings and royalty
in foreign lands long before she could sing for
                                                 thee,
the segregated American, united musically.

On pitch-perfect notes, Marian sang of
                                                 we,
to a country divided by
the definition of equality.

Caged by color, the songbird took wing
and America's spirit soared
when it heard Marian
                                                 sing.

Marian Anderson was scheduled to perform at Constitution Hall in Washington DC for a group called the Daughters of the American Revolution. When the group refused permission for Marian to sing to an integrated audience, one of their members, First Lady Eleanor Roosevelt, resigned and invited her to perform at the Lincoln Memorial. Marian's opening song was, "My Country 'Tis of Thee."

Day 14

April 15, 1947 Jackie Robinson
First African-American to play in a Major League Baseball game.

Pigeon-toed feet
in well-traveled cleats
step onto the field
ready to compete.

Blue socks rise
under bright white pants
of the rookie first baseman
with the bat in his hands.

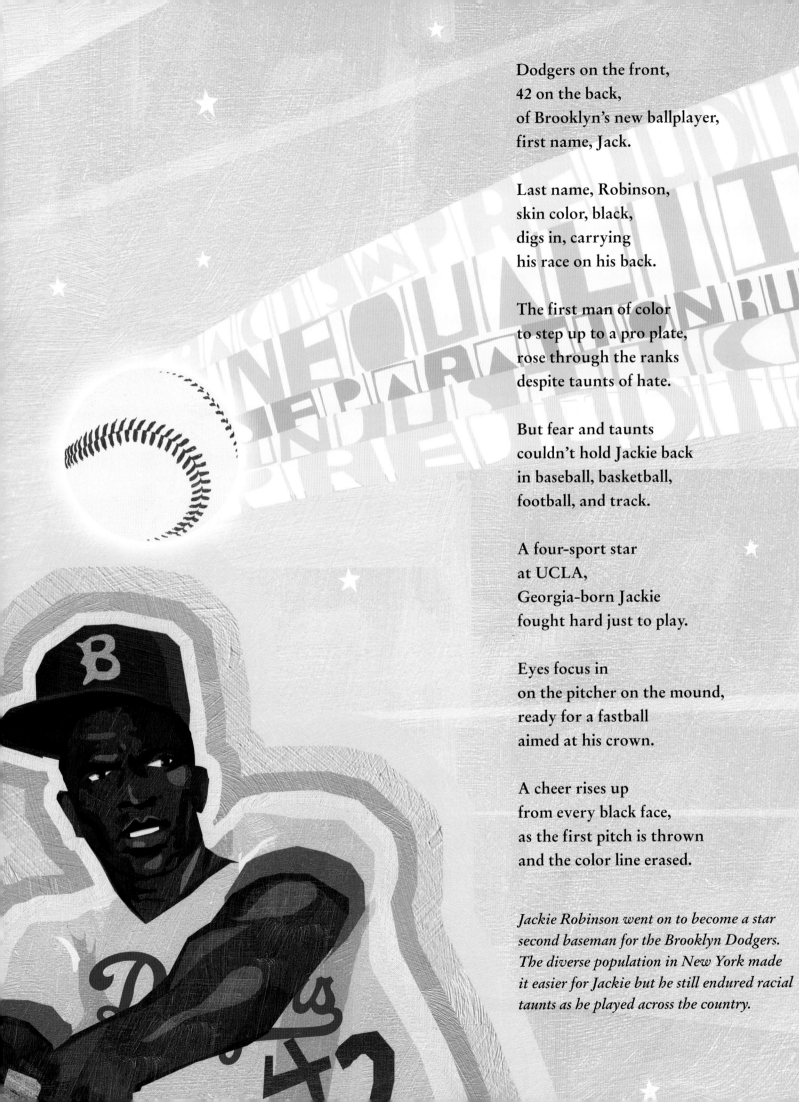

Dodgers on the front,
42 on the back,
of Brooklyn's new ballplayer,
first name, Jack.

Last name, Robinson,
skin color, black,
digs in, carrying
his race on his back.

The first man of color
to step up to a pro plate,
rose through the ranks
despite taunts of hate.

But fear and taunts
couldn't hold Jackie back
in baseball, basketball,
football, and track.

A four-sport star
at UCLA,
Georgia-born Jackie
fought hard just to play.

Eyes focus in
on the pitcher on the mound,
ready for a fastball
aimed at his crown.

A cheer rises up
from every black face,
as the first pitch is thrown
and the color line erased.

Jackie Robinson went on to become a star
second baseman for the Brooklyn Dodgers.
The diverse population in New York made
it easier for Jackie but he still endured racial
taunts as he played across the country.

Day 15

May 17, 1954 *Brown v. Board of Education*
decision, eliminating segregation in schools.

"We conc ude that n the field of public educatio , the octrine of 'sep rate but equal' has no place. Separate educational facilities are inherently unequal."

—United States Supreme Court

When Oliver Brown of Topeka, Kansas, tried to enroll his daughter in the nearest school, just seven blocks away, he was told it was for white children only. To get to the black school, his daughter would have to walk a mile through a railroad switchyard. Her name was   . Her case and many others like it were filed under one claim and questioned if schools could truly be "separate but equal."

Day 16

December 1, 1955 Rosa Parks sits.

With tired feet and courage in her eyes,
on a bus in Montgomery, Alabama,
Rosa sat, so others could rise.

Christmas lights lit up the December skies
as a fatigued soul sat still
with tired feet and courage in her eyes.

Black faces obeyed with swallowed sighs
when told "move to the back,"
but Rosa sat, so others could rise.

Police made an arrest when there was no reply
from the seamstress with spectacles,
with tired feet and courage in her eyes.

To jail, with eyes focused on freedom's prize,
the color line was questioned when
Rosa sat, so others could rise.

Standing up to injustice
by taking a seat,
with tired feet and courage in her eyes,
Rosa Parks sat, so others could rise.

*Rosa Parks inspired the civil rights movement. When her
story spread across Montgomery, a boycott of Birmingham
buses was organized by a young minister by the name of
Martin Luther King Jr.*

Day 17

May 26, 1956 Althea Gibson
becomes first black woman to win a tennis title.

August 25, 1968 Arthur Ashe
becomes first black man to win a tennis title.

Althea	Gibson
Arthur	Ashe
champions	in tennis
champions	with class.
Althea,	raised
in Harlem	NYC,
first	became
a paddle tennis	prodigy.
Arthur,	born
in Richmond	VA,
was six	when tennis
called him	to play.
Althea	progressed
from paddle	to racquet
and learned	to chase
the ball	and smack it.
Arthur	progressed
on the court	fast
and hit	the books hard,
becoming first	in his class.
Althea	and Arthur
soon began	to win,
not once	not twice
but again	and again.

But Althea and Arthur
were shut out of play
with white players in big tournaments
until one fine day.

The stage, the French Open
where Althea became
the first black champion
in the pro tennis game.

Twelve years later,
Arthur held in his hand
the US Open trophy
as the best in the land.

Like Jackie Robinson before,
Althea Gibson and Arthur Ashe
erased the color line
with hard work and class.

Althea Gibson was born in South Carolina on August 25, 1927, but moved to New York City when she was three. She took up tennis at the age of fourteen and would eventually go on to also win Wimbledon twice and the US Open twice, earning her a total of five grand slam (major tennis) titles.

Arthur Ashe was born July 10, 1943, in Richmond, Virginia. He was valedictorian in his high school and turned pro at the age of twenty-six. In addition to winning the US Open, he went on to win Wimbledon and would go on to become the first black tennis player to be ranked number one in the world.

Day 18

September 25, 1957 **"Little Rock Nine"** attend classes in Little Rock's Central High School under the protection of the U.S. Army's 101st Airborne Division.

Day 1

Nine fresh faces,
wide-eyed and black,
tried to enter Central High
but National Guards kept them back.

One was separated
wearing dark sunglasses
hiding tears of fear
as white faces harassed her.

Bayonets greeted them
and turned them away
as a chant rang out
from the chaos to say:

"2-4-6-8, we don't wanna integrate!"
"2-4-6-8, we don't wanna integrate!"

Day 2

Two weeks later,
no guards, just a crowd,
about one thousand strong
stood hostile and loud.

Through a side door
the students slipped through, quiet,
but news of their entry
caused a near riot.

Trapped in the school
police smuggled them away
in cars through a mob
with guns on display.

Day 3

The next day, the president
put Little Rock in line
by sending troops to protect
the Little Rock Nine.

Helicopters and soldiers
created an atmosphere of war
as the new students
were escorted to the door.

Nine brave teenagers
dealt a blow to segregation
when they ascended the steps
to an equal education.

When it was learned that nine black students would
attempt to enter segregated Central High in Little
Rock, Arkansas, the governor ordered the National
Guard to keep them out. The students were chosen
from area schools because of their good grades and
included: Ernest Green, Elizabeth Eckford, Jefferson
Thomas, Terrence Roberts, Carlotta Walls, Minniejean
Brown, Gloria Ray, Thelma Mothershed, and Melba
Pattillo. Rather than be forced to integrate, the
governor closed all schools the following year.

Day 19

September 11, 1960
Wilma Rudolph wins third Olympic gold medal.

1940, June 23,
a child is born
in St. Bethlehem, Tennessee.

A sickly child
born two months early,
just four and a half pounds
but a bundle of energy.

Nineteen siblings
all tried to relieve her
as she battled pneumonia,
measles, and scarlet fever.

Then came polio
and a heartbreaking talk
when doctors said
the child would never again walk.

But visits to a hospital
fifty miles away,
twice a week and
leg massages every day,
brought the leg back to life
and allowed the child to play.

First came basketball,
then came track,
then came the Olympics
and the wind at her back.

With legs like a gazelle
powered by the heart of a lion,
Wilma Rudolph took gold
with a will strong as iron.

Wilma Rudolph was the first American female track athlete to win three Olympic gold medals in a single Olympics. In Rome, 1960, she set Olympic records in the 100- and 200-meter races and a world record in the 4x100 relay, where she was the anchor. Four years earlier, at the age of sixteen, she earned an Olympic bronze medal as part of the 4x100 relay team.

Day 20

August 28, 1963 March on Washington, **Martin Luther King Jr.** delivers "I Have a Dream" speech.

On buses, they came.
On trains, they came.
In cars, they came.
On planes, they came.
By foot, they came.

To march.

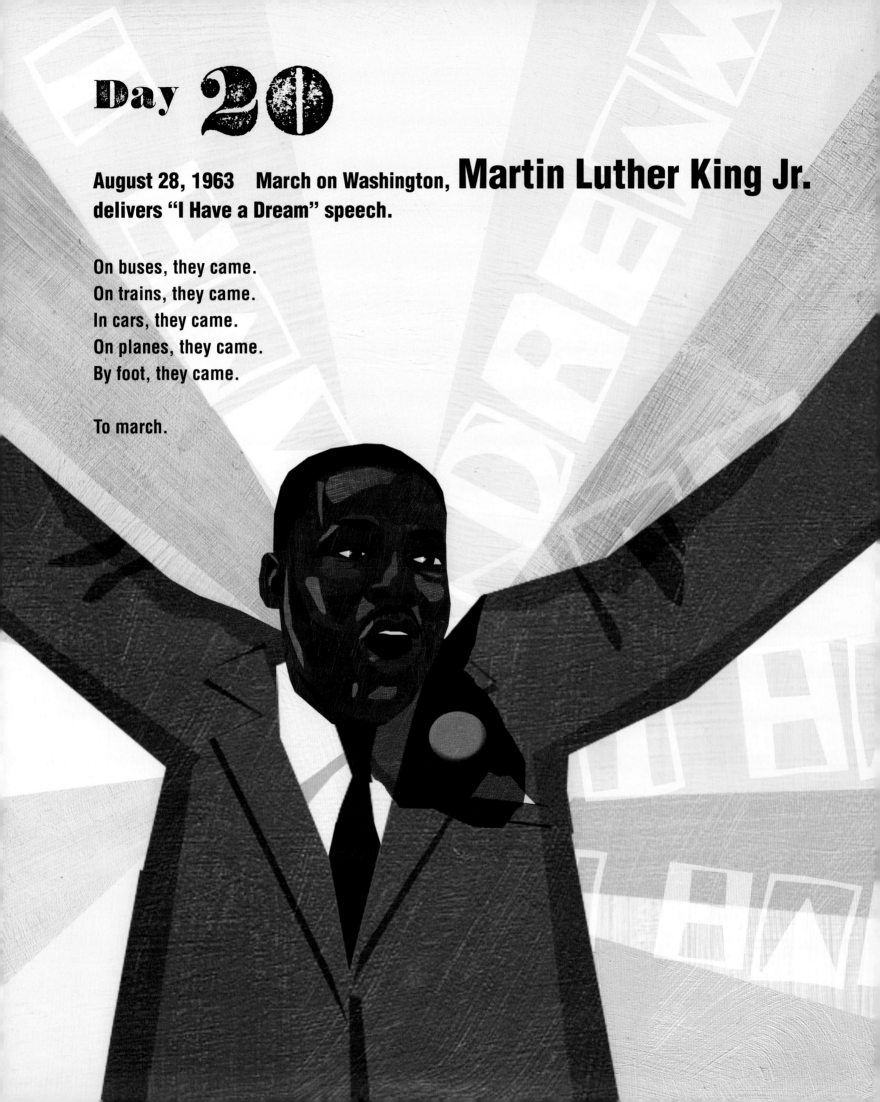

With blisters on their feet,
they came.
With purpose in their step,
they came.
With strength in their spirit,
they came.
With hope in their heart,
they came.

To march.

Old faces.
Young faces.
Black faces.
White faces.
Marched.
And gathered.
And listened.

Standing small beneath Lincoln,
standing tall above the crowd, one voice spoke:

"I have a dream . . ."

And the world listened.

Over 200,000 people participated in the March on Washington for Jobs and Freedom, but with the power of TV and radio, it was broadcast to the world. Various black leaders spoke throughout the day before Martin Luther King Jr. ended with his now famous speech. A year later the Civil Rights Act was passed, ending segregation.

Day 21

Black,

fier**y**

and

never

yielding,

Malcolm X

electrified

m**a**sses

by preachi**n**g

self-respect,

i**n**telligence,

fr**e**edom,

a**c**tion,

d**e**votion,

di**s**cipline, and

self-determination,

m**a**king him

a dange**r**ous

revolutionar**y**.

Malcolm X, born Malcolm Little, stepped into the public eye as a minister for the Nation of Islam, which became labeled as the Black Muslim movement. The Nation's leader, Elijah Muhammad, preached education and self-determination, among other things, to its members. But before Malcolm was introduced to the Nation of Islam, he made some bad choices that ultimately landed him in prison. Malcolm used his prison sentence to educate himself by reading books and joining the debate team. Upon his release, he put his words to work by giving speeches for the Nation to attract new members. Where Martin Luther King Jr. preached nonviolence, Malcolm X had a different point of view that focused on standing up to injustice, "by any means necessary."

Day 22

October 2, 1967 Thurgood Marshall

sworn in as first black Supreme Court justice.

"I, Thurgood Marshall, do solemnly swear or affirm that I will administer justice without respect to persons, and do equal right to the poor and to the rich, and that I will faithfully and impartially discharge and perform all the duties incumbent upon me as Associate Justice of the United States Supreme Court, according to the best of my abilities and understanding, agreeably to the constitution and laws of the United States. So help me God."

As a young boy, Thurgood Marshall was taught an appreciation for the Constitution and the law by his father. He went on to receive a law degree from Howard University where he was encouraged by a mentor to apply the Constitution to overturn unjust laws. He was successful in getting the first black student admitted to the University of Maryland Law School, a school that also rejected Marshall because of his color. He argued Brown v. Board of Education and won, and overturned case after case throughout the country to end segregation before joining the Supreme Court.

Day 23

January 25, 1972 Shirley Chisholm declares herself as a presidential candidate for the Democratic Party—the first black woman ever to do so.

Run Shirley Run
for New York State Assembly!

Go Shirley Go
for U.S. Congress!

Win Shirley Win
to become the president!

Vote Shirley Chisholm,
a woman for the people,
unbought and unbossed!

Shirley Chisholm became interested in politics when a political science professor at Brooklyn College suggested she had a natural talent for it. Shirley was born in Brooklyn, New York, but lived from age three to ten in Barbados, a former British colony. There, she received a well-rounded education that made her a top student upon her return to New York, eventually earning several college scholarships. Throughout her career as a politician, Shirley spoke out for minorities and women. Her campaign slogan when running for president was "Unbought and Unbossed," to remind everyone that Shirley Chisholm was her own woman.

Day 24

April 8, 1974 **Hank Aaron** hits his 715th home run, breaking Babe Ruth's long-standing career home run record.

Hack away Hank
get a hit
get a ribbie.
Hack away Hank
hack away at history.

Gehrig,
Williams,
Mantle,
all fell
as Hank hacked away
to left, right,
and center field.

Hank kept hacking
and soon took aim
at the home run record
with Babe Ruth's name.

Tied with Willie Mays,
Hank hacked for the crown
and blasted a slider
that took the Babe down.

The stadium exploded
into chants and cheers
as black faces flowed
with pride and tears.

Hank (born Henry) Aaron took the home run record from Babe Ruth in his twentieth year in the league. As he got closer to the record, he and his family received hate mail and death threats because of his race. When fans heard about this they countered with letters of support, which pushed Hank harder to achieve the record. As of this writing, Barry Bonds has since taken the home run record, but Hank still holds the record for most RBIs ("runs batted in" aka "ribbies").

Day 25

August 30, 1983 Guion "Guy" Bluford becomes first black astronaut launched into space aboard the space shuttle *Challenger*.

September 12, 1992 Mae Jemison becomes first black female astronaut in space aboard the space shuttle *Endeavour*.

10

As a young boy, **Guion "Guy" Bluford** enjoys building model airplanes and dreams of one day building real ones.

Mae Jemison is born in the tenth month, October, on the 17th in 1956.

Guy Bluford logged 688 hours in space and retired from NASA and the Air Force in 1993. He was inducted into the International Space Hall of Fame in 1998.

Mae Jemison logged 190 hours in space on her only mission. She left NASA in 1993 to pursue a private career in the sciences.

9

Guy is born on November 22, 1942, nine months after the Tuskegee Airmen become the first all-black flying unit. Ninth grade, **Mae** enters high school at age twelve.

5

Guy is one of five astronauts on board the space shuttle *Challenger*. Age five, **Mae** declares she wants to be a scientist when she grows up.

"Don't you mean a nurse?" her kindergarten teacher says.

"No, I mean a scientist," Mae says.

8

Guy is chosen as part of NASA Group 8, the first class of orbiting space shuttle astronauts. Some 8,000 applied, 35 were accepted, including Guy and two other black astronauts. **Mae** begins taking dance class at eight years old. Learns she is afraid of heights when taking the elevated train to class in Chicago.

4

Guy has four college degrees: a bachelor's, master's, and doctorate in aerospace engineering, and a master of business administration. Fourth grade, **Mae** cuts her hair into a short Afro. Since not many had the hairstyle and she was tall, she was often confused for a boy.

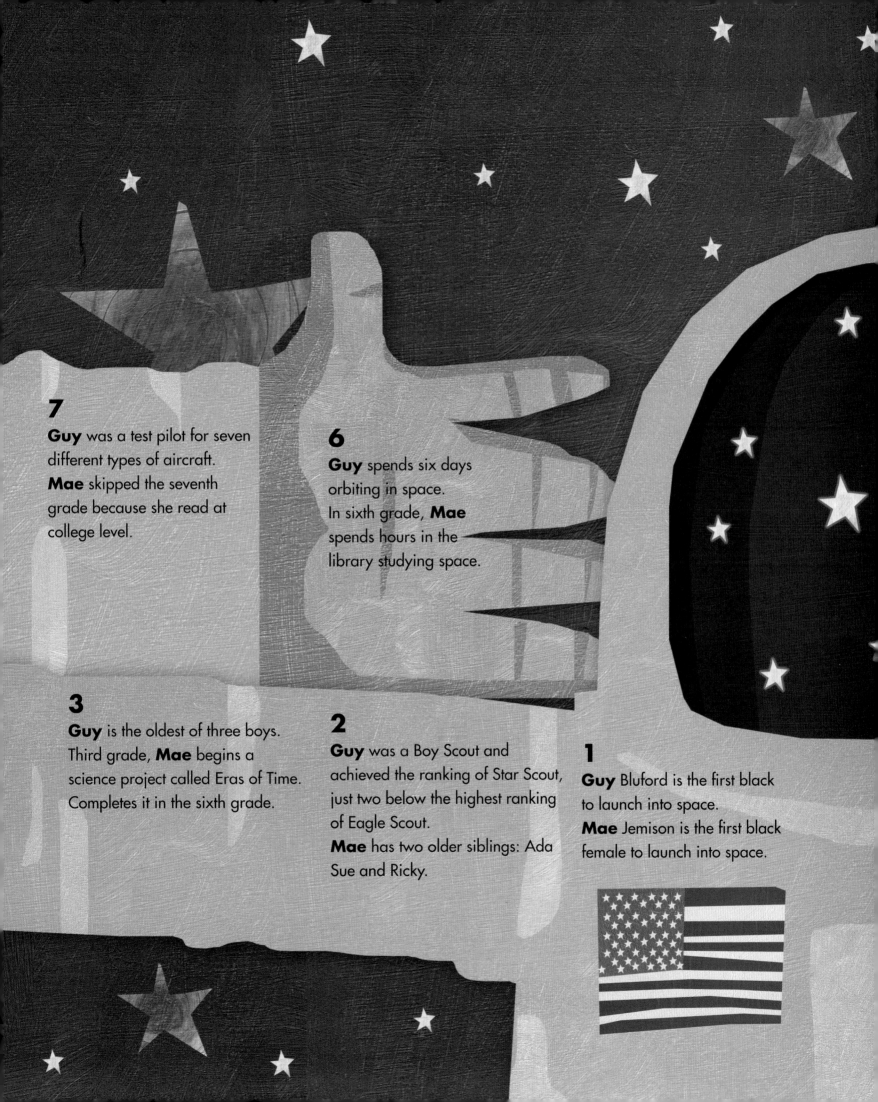

7

Guy was a test pilot for seven different types of aircraft. **Mae** skipped the seventh grade because she read at college level.

6

Guy spends six days orbiting in space. In sixth grade, **Mae** spends hours in the library studying space.

3

Guy is the oldest of three boys. Third grade, **Mae** begins a science project called Eras of Time. Completes it in the sixth grade.

2

Guy was a Boy Scout and achieved the ranking of Star Scout, just two below the highest ranking of Eagle Scout. **Mae** has two older siblings: Ada Sue and Ricky.

1

Guy Bluford is the first black to launch into space. **Mae** Jemison is the first black female to launch into space.

Day **26**

May 10, 1994
Nelson Mandela
inaugurated as first black
president of South Africa.

Man-de-la!
Man-de-la!
Man of the people
Man-de-la!

Ma-di-ba!
Ma-di-ba!
Son of Africa
Ma-di-ba!

South African president
Man-de-la!

Nelson Mandela was sentenced
to life in prison in June 1964 when found guilty
of trying to cause a violent revolution in South Africa. This was
due to his work with the African National Congress (ANC), a group that supports
the rights of native Africans. In 1948, apartheid (separateness) went into effect
in South Africa, creating laws that caused inequality between whites and
blacks. Mandela was given many chances at freedom if he agreed to stop
his work with the ANC but he declined each time. With the eyes of the world
focused on South Africa's brutal policies, President F. W. de Klerk began
releasing political prisoners including Mandela. The two men then worked
to create a constitution and shared government for all South Africans. As
a member of the Madiba clan, many took to calling him that as a nickname.

Day

February 27, 2003 *Forbes* magazine declares **Oprah Winfrey** first black female billionaire in world history.

1—Oprah Gail Winfrey born to a single mother.

10—Bounced between mother and father in Milwaukee and Nashville.

100—Out of control child moves in with disciplined father. Father requires a book report a week; she becomes an honor student.

1,000—Full scholarship earned to Tennessee State University to study speech communications and performing arts.

10,000—Bubbling radio personality in Nashville becomes TV news coanchor in Baltimore.

100,000—Awkward coanchor blossoms as outgoing talk show cohost.

1 Million—Cohost in Baltimore becomes host in Chicago.

10 Million—Chicago talk show host becomes movie star in *The Color Purple*.

100 Million—Movie star becomes TV star when talk show goes to national audience.

1 Billion—Host plus actress plus TV producer plus film producer plus magazine publisher equals Harpo Productions; Oprah spelled backward. From Oprah Winfrey to Oprah to just O.

Oprah Gail Winfrey was born in Kosciusko, Mississippi. Her grandmother raised her early on and taught her to read at a young age. Ever since she was three, Oprah shared her gift for performing and connecting with people. It began in local churches where she recited Bible verses. It progressed in high school where she competed in drama recitals. Her positive outlook on life came from overcoming many personal obstacles, which she shared on TV. Like Madam C. J. Walker before her, Oprah works just as hard at giving her money away as she does earning it. She opened a girls' school in South Africa and donates money to individuals who help others.

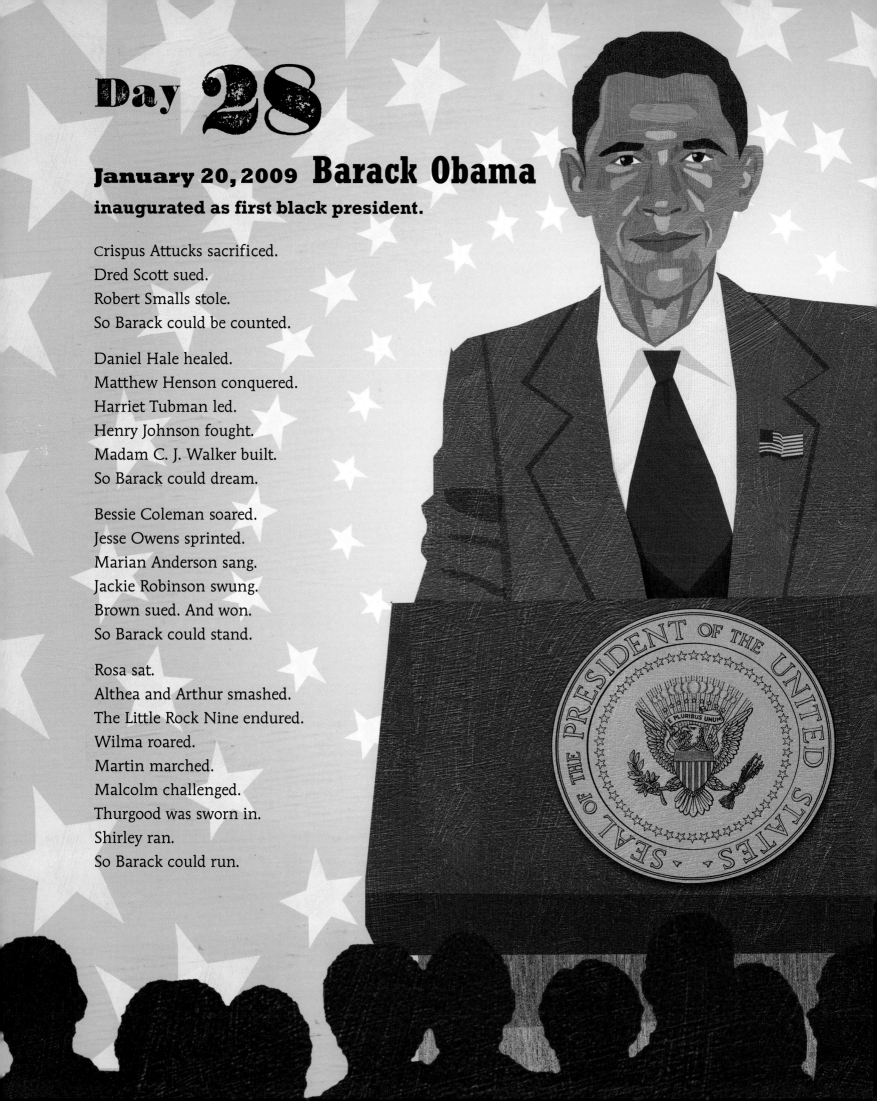

Day 28

January 20, 2009 Barack Obama
inaugurated as first black president.

Crispus Attucks sacrificed.
Dred Scott sued.
Robert Smalls stole.
So Barack could be counted.

Daniel Hale healed.
Matthew Henson conquered.
Harriet Tubman led.
Henry Johnson fought.
Madam C. J. Walker built.
So Barack could dream.

Bessie Coleman soared.
Jesse Owens sprinted.
Marian Anderson sang.
Jackie Robinson swung.
Brown sued. And won.
So Barack could stand.

Rosa sat.
Althea and Arthur smashed.
The Little Rock Nine endured.
Wilma roared.
Martin marched.
Malcolm challenged.
Thurgood was sworn in.
Shirley ran.
So Barack could run.

Hank hacked away.
Mae and Guy launched.
Mandela inspired.
Oprah earned.
So Barack could win.

Number forty-four, America's first black president.

*Barack Hussein Obama was born on August 4, 1961, in Honolulu, Hawaii. His
mother was a white woman from Kansas and his father a black man from Kenya,
Africa. Barack was called Barry for years because he had no true connection to
his African name, but that changed when he attended Columbia University. As
a college student he embraced his name and mixed heritage. Upon graduation he
moved to Chicago to work as a community organizer, then left to attend Harvard
Law School. He felt that even though he was able to help people, a law degree would
allow him to help even more. Eventually he returned to Chicago to work again as
an organizer but then entered politics where he began his career as an Illinois state
senator. Eight years later he became a U.S. Senator and just four years later became
president of the United States.*

Day 29

Today

What will today bring,
what will today be,
will today be the day
you make history?

Will your thoughts evolve science,
will your skill earn gold,
will your life story be
one worth being told?

Will your questions change laws,
will your words inspire others,
will your name be passed on
by fathers and mothers?

Will the fire in your spirit
spark a revolution,
will your actions advance
humanity's evolution?

Will others follow you into battle
to defend liberty,
will today be the day
you add to history?

Today is the day,
today is to be.

Bibliography

Bell, Susan, Jacquie Jones & Nolan Walker (dir.), *Africans in America: America's Journey Through Slavery*, DVD. WGBH Boston: 2000.

Carney Smith, Jessie & Linda T. Wynn, *Freedom Facts and Firsts: 400 Years of the African American Civil Rights Experience*. Visible Ink Press: 2009.

Ferguson Delano, Marfe, *American Heroes: Fifty Profiles of Great Americans*. National Geographic Society: 2005.

Frankel, Noralee, *Break Those Chains at Last: African Americans 1860–1880*, Young Oxford History of African Americans, vol. 5. Oxford University Press: 1996.

Gates, Jr., Henry Louis, *Life Upon These Shores: Looking at African American History, 1513–2008*. Knopf, 2011

Gormley, Beatrice, *Malcolm X: A Revolutionary Voice*. Sterling Publishisng: 2008.

Halfmann, Janet, *Seven Miles to Freedom: The Robert Smalls Story*. Lee & Low: 2008.

Jemison, Mae, *Find Where The Wind Goes: Moments from My Life*. Scholastic Press: 2001.

Johnson, Dolores, *Onward: A Photobiography of African-American Polar Explorer Matthew Henson*. National Geographic Society: 2005.

Kramer, Anne, *Mandela: The Rebel Who Led His Nation to Freedom*. National Geographic Society, 2005

Krull, Kathleen & David Diaz, *Wilma Unlimited: How Wilma Rudolph Became the World's Fastest Woman*. HMH Books for Young Readers: 2000.

Lasky, Kathryn & Nneka Bennett, *Vision of Beauty: The Story of Sarah Breedlove Walker*. Candlewick Press, 2000.

Marks, Jennifer L., *President Barack Obama*. Pebble Plus/Capstone Press: 2009.

McWhorter , Diane, *A Dream of Freedom: The Civil Rights Movement from 1954 to 1968*. Scholastic: 2004.

Plantz, Connie, *Bessie Coleman: First Black Woman Pilot*. Enslow Publishers: 2001.

Tavares, Matt, *Henry Aaron's Dream*. Candlewick Press: 2010.

TIME for Kids editors with Renée Skelton, *Harriet Tubman: A Woman of Courage*. HarperCollins: 2005.

Young, Jeff C., *Brilliant African-American Scientists: Nine Exceptional Lives*. Myreportlinks.com Books/Enslow Publishers, Inc.: 2009.